THE
LOVELINESS
OF CHRIST

THE
LOVELINESS
OF CHRIST

SELECTIONS *from the* LETTERS *of*
SAMUEL RUTHERFORD

SELECTED *by* ELLEN S. LISTER

INTRODUCED *by* JIM *&* BESSIE WILSON

COMMUNITY CHRISTIAN MINISTRIES
MOSCOW, IDAHO

Published by Community Christian Ministries
P.O. Box 9754, Moscow, Idaho 83843
208.883.0997 | www.ccmbooks.org

Samuel Rutherford, *The Loveliness of Christ: Selections from the Letters of Samuel Rutherford*. Originally printed by Samuel Bagster & Sons, London, 1909. Reprinted with permission.
Preface copyright © 1990, 2018 by Jim Wilson and Bessie Wilson

Cover design by James Engerbretson.
Interior design by Valerie Anne Bost.
Cover photo by Hannah K. Grieser, etsy.com/shop/Aperturity.
Printed in the United States of America.

18 19 20 21 22 23 24 25   9 8 7 6 5 4 3 2 1

CONTENTS

FOREWORD

YOU CAN TELL THAT MY WIFE, Bessie, carried her copy of *The Loveliness of Christ* with her for many years. In celebration of our twenty-five years together, we were in London, England, in 1977. I made a special trip to Samuel Bagster & Sons to get more copies for her to give to friends. The booklet was out of print, and there was no intention to reprint it. So at that time, I obtained permission to reprint it.

With gratefulness to our special friends for whom this was first republished,

JIM WILSON
Moscow, Idaho
2018

PREFACE

WHEN WE READ *THE LOVELINESS of Christ*, it is as though a curtain is raised for us, enabling us to observe a man so taken up with his Lord that we want to kneel with him. It is not a book to read straight through, but to graze in, appropriating what we need, going back during a trial and seeing what we missed on our first reading. It is a book to mark in, as I did, with "so true," and, "Lord, let it be my experience too." We send it out hoping it will bless and strengthen you.

Anne Cousin wrote a seventeen-stanza hymn called "The Sands of Time are Sinking" using phrases from the letters of Samuel Rutherford. Here we reprint two of those stanzas; you may recognize some phrases as you read through *The Loveliness of Christ.*

BESSIE WILSON
Moscow, Idaho
1990

The sands of time are sinking,
The dawn of heaven breaks
The Summer morn I've sighed for,
The fair sweet morn awakes.

Dark, dark hath been the midnight,
But dayspring is at hand,
And glory, glory dwelleth
In Emmanuel's land.

The Bride eyes not her garment,
But her dear bridegroom's face;
I will not gaze at glory,
But on my King of grace;
Not at the crown He giveth
But on His pierced hand.
The Lamb is all the glory
Of Emmanuel's land.

BIOGRAPHICAL
BACKGROUND

SAMUEL RUTHERFORD WAS BORN about the year 1600 in the Borders of Scotland. At the age of seventeen, he entered Edinburgh College, where he received his Master of Arts Degree in 1621. Soon after, he was appointed Professor of Humanity, which position he held until 1625. Then for two years he studied on his own, mostly in the area of theology.

We have no evidence that he was converted in early life. We have a suggestion from his writings that he was converted as an adult. "Like a fool as I was, I suffered my sun to be high in the heaven, and near afternoon, before I ever took the gate by the end."

In 1627, Rutherford took a church in southwestern Scotland near the Firth of Solway. He pastored there with little fruit among the common people, although he labored night and day for nine years. However, there was fruit among the educated. His writings and preaching began to get attention. His voice was shrill and his elocution poor; however, according to Woodrow's Church History, he was "one of the most moving and affectionate preachers in his time, or perhaps in any age of the church." And from another source, "Many times I thought he would have flown out of the pulpit when he came to speak of Jesus Christ" (MacCrie's Sketches).[1]

He had a great burden for the lost. "I would lay my dearest joys in the gap between you and eternal destruction," and, "My witness is in heaven, your heaven would be two heavens to me, and your salvation, two salvations."

He wrote 220 letters in a two-year period when he was in exile in Aberdeen for refusing to sign the Acts of Episcopacy and for his writings against the Arminians. Although he was not in prison, he was not allowed to leave the city.

In 1638, he became a Professor of Divinity and later a Principal at the University of St. Andrews. In 1643, he was one of the Commissioners from the Church of Scotland to the

---

1 Thomas M'Crie, "The First Martyrs of the Covenant," in *Scottish Christian Herald, Volume I, January 5–December 28, 1839* (Edinburgh: John Johnstone, 1839) 773.

Westminster Assembly. There is evidence that he was the author of the Shorter Catechism.

In 1651, Scotland crowned Charles II as lawful king at Scone. When Charles was at St. Andrews in anticipation of the coronation, he visited the colleges. It fell to Samuel Rutherford to deliver an oration in Latin before the prospective king. The title was "The Duty of Kings." This was well thought out, for eight years before he had written *Lex, Rex*, subtitled *The Law and the Prince*, a central point of which is that even kings are under the law of God. This same work, under the same king, in 1661, caused him to be summoned to be tried before the Scottish Parliament on a charge of High Treason.

Prior to this, *Lex, Rex* had been burned by the hangman in Edinburgh, and a few days later by a bishop under the windows of Rutherford's college in St. Andrews.

Rutherford was on his deathbed when he received the summons. He sent this reply, "I behove to answer my first summons; and ere your day arrive, I will be where few kings and great folks appear."

On the afternoon of March 29, 1661, he said, "This night will close the door, and fasten my anchor within the veil, and I shall go away in sleep by five o'clock in the morning." He died at five o'clock in the morning March 30, 1661. His last words before he went to sleep were, "Glory, glory dwelleth in Immanuel's land."

His first wife died before she was thirty. His two children were taken from him. He married again at forty and had seven children, six of whom died before he did.

Although he entered into controversy, you can tell by his letters that Rutherford was not an angry or bitter controversialist.

His enemies, by contrast, did become angry and hateful towards him. In this sense, he was like the Lord Jesus Christ, who was also a controversialist. In our day, we do not know how to enter necessary controversy without the passions which so frequently result in sin. We offer this small book to the public in the hope that we would all learn something of Rutherford's Christlike balance.

THE LOVELINESS
OF CHRIST

THE GREAT MASTER GARDENER, the Father of our Lord Jesus Christ, in a wonderful providence,[2] with His own hand, planted me here, where by His grace, in this part of His vineyard, I grow; and here I will abide till the great Master of the vineyard think fit to transplant me.

2 provision, supply

IF YOUR LORD CALL YOU TO suffering, be not dismayed; there shall be a new allowance of the King for you when ye come to it. One of the softest pillows Christ hath is laid under His witnesses' head, though often they must set down their bare feet among thorns.

GOD HATH CALLED YOU TO Christ's side, and the wind is now in Christ's face in this land; and seeing ye are with Him, ye cannot expect the lee-side or the sunny side of the brae.[3]

HE DELIGHTETH TO TAKE UP fallen bairns[4] and to mend broken brows: binding up of wounds is His office.

3 hillside, hill, any slope
4 children

WANTS[5] ARE MY BEST RICHES, FOR I have these supplied by Christ.

I HOPE TO OVER-HOPE AND OVER-believe my troubles.

I THINK THE SENSE OF OUR wants, when withal we have a restlessness and a sort of spiritual impatience under them, and can make a din, because we want Him whom our soul loveth, is that which maketh an open door to Christ: and when we think we are going backward, because we feel deadness, we are going forward; for the more sense the more life, and no sense argueth no life.

THERE IS NO SWEETER FELLOW ship with Christ than to bring our wounds and our sores to Him.

5 needs

THERE IS AS MUCH IN OUR LORD'S
pantry as will satisfy all His bairns, and as
much wine in His cellar as will quench all
their thirst. Hunger on; for there is meat
in hunger for Christ: go never from Him,
but fash[6] Him (who yet is pleased with the
importunity of hungry souls) with a dish-
ful of hungry desires, till He fill you; and
if He delay yet come not ye away, albeit[7] ye
should fall a-swoon at His feet.

I FIND IT MOST TRUE, THAT THE
greatest temptation out of hell is to live
without temptations; if my waters should
stand, they would rot. Faith is the better of
the free air, and of the sharp winter storm
in its face. Grace withereth without adver-
sity. The devil is but God's master fencer, to
teach us to handle our weapons.

6 vex, importune, pester
7 although

O, PITY FOR EVERMORE THAT there should be such an one as Christ Jesus, so boundless, so bottomless, and so incomparable in infinite excellency, and sweetness, and so few to take Him! O, ye poor dry dead souls, why will ye not come hither with your toom[8] vessels and your empty souls to this huge, and fair, and deep, and sweet well of life, and fill all your toom vessels?

O, THAT CHRIST SHOULD BE SO large in sweetness and worth, and we so narrow, pinched, so ebb,[9] and so void of all happiness, and yet men will not take Him! they lose their love miserably, who will not bestow it upon this lovely One.

---

8 empty
9 shallow, backward flowing

I KNOW ALL CREATED POWER
should sink under me if I should lean
down upon it, and therefore it is better to
rest on God than sink or fall; and we weak
souls must have a bottom and being-place,
for we cannot stand out alone. Let us then
be wise in our choice and choose and wail
our own blessedness, which is to trust in
the Lord.

THEY ARE NOT LOST TO YOU THAT
are laid up in Christ's treasury in heaven.
At the resurrection ye shall meet with
them: there they are, sent before but not
sent away. Your Lord loveth you, who is
homely to take and give, borrow and lend.

YE WILL NOT GET LEAVE TO STEAL
quietly to heaven, in Christ's company,
without a conflict and a cross.

I FIND CROSSES CHRIST'S CARVED work that He marketh out for us, and that with crosses He figureth and portrayeth us to His own image, cutting away pieces of our ill and corruption. Lord cut, Lord carve, Lord wound, Lord do anything that may perfect Thy Father's image in us, and make us meet for glory.

IT IS THE LORD'S KINDNESS THAT He will take the scum off us in the fire. Who knoweth how needful winnowing is to us, and what dross we must want ere we enter into the kingdom of God? So narrow is the entry to heaven, that our knots, our bunches and lumps of pride, and self-love, and idol-love, and world-love must be hammered off us, that we may throng in, stooping low, and creeping through that narrow and thorny entry.

O, WHAT OWE I TO THE FILE, TO THE hammer, to the furnace of my Lord Jesus!

WHY SHOULD I START AT[10] THE plough of my Lord, that maketh deep furrows on my soul? I know He is no idle husbandman; He purposeth a crop.

CROSSES ARE PROCLAIMED AS common accidents to all the saints, and in them standeth a part of our communion with Christ.

HOW SWEET A THING WERE IT FOR us to learn to make our burdens light by framing our hearts to the burden, and making our Lord's will a law.

10 be surprised by, be afraid of

IT IS NOT THE SUNNY SIDE OF
Christ that we must look to, and we must
not forsake Him for want of that; but must
set our face against what may befall us, in
following on, till He and we through the
briers and bushes on the dry ground. Our
soft nature would be borne through the
troubles of this miserable life in Christ's
arms. And it is His wisdom, who knoweth
our mould, that His bairns go wet-shod
and cold-footed to heaven.

THERE IS NOTHING BUT PERFECT
garden-flowers in heaven, and the best
plenishing that is there is Christ.

IT IS NOT A SMOOTH AND EASY
way, neither will your weather be fair and
pleasant; but whosoever saw the invisible
God and the fair city, makes no reckoning

of losses or crosses. In ye must be, cost you what it will; stand not for a price, and for all that ye have, to win[11] the castle; the rights of it are won to you, and it is disponed[12] to you, in your Lord Jesus's Testament; and see what a fair legacy your dying Friend, Christ, hath left you: and there wanteth nothing but possession.

O! MEN'S SOULS HAVE NO WINGS, and therefore night and day they keep their nest and are not acquaint with Christ.

WHAT CAN I SAY OF HIM? LET US go and see.

I HAVE LITTLE, LITTLE OF HIM; yet I long for more.

11   get, make one's way
12   made over, disposed of property in one's will (Scottish law)

SCAR[13] NOT AT SUFFERING FOR Christ: for Christ hath a chair, and a cushion, and sweet peace for a sufferer.

HE TAKETH THE BAIRNS IN HIS arms when they come to a deep water; at least, when they lose ground, and are put to swim, then His hand is under their chin.

MY SHALLOW AND EBB THOUGHTS are not the compass Christ saileth by. I leave His ways to Himself, for they are far, far above me . . . There are windings and to's and fro's in His ways, which blind bodies like us cannot see.

I SEE GRACE GROWETH BEST IN winter.

13 be scared

I KNOW, WE MAY SAY, THAT Christ is kindest in His love when we are at our weakest; and that if Christ had not been to the fore, in our sad days, the waters had gone over our soul.

I VERILY JUDGE, WE KNOW NOT how much may be had in this life: there is yet something beyond all we see, that seeking would light upon.

LET HIM MAKE ANYTHING OUT of me, so being He be glorified in my salvation: for I know I am made for Him.

MEN DO LOP THE BRANCHES OFF their trees round about, to the end they may grow up high and tall. The Lord hath this way lopped your branch, in taking from you many children, to the end ye should grow upward, like one of the Lord's cedars.

POOR FOLKS MUST EITHER BORROW or beg from the rich, and the only thing that commendeth sinners to Christ is extreme necessity and want. Christ's love is ready to make and provide a ransom and money for a poor body who hath lost his purse. "Ho, ye that have no money, come and buy" (Isaiah 55:1). That is the poor man's market.

EVERY DAY WE MAY SEE SOME new thing in Christ. His love hath neither brim nor bottom.

GO WHERE YE WILL, YOUR SOUL shall not sleep sound but in Christ's bosom.

I FIND THAT OUR WANTS QUALIFY us for Christ.

MY DEAR BROTHER, I WILL THINK
it comfort if ye speak my name to our Well-
Beloved wherever you are. I am mindful
of you.

I BLESS YOU FOR YOUR PRAYERS; ADD
to them praises. As I am able, I pay you home.

BLESSED WERE WE IF WE COULD
make ourselves masters of that invaluable
treasure, the love of Christ; or rather suffer ourselves to be mastered and subdued
to Christ's love, so as Christ were our all
things, and all other things our nothings,
and the refuse of our delights. O, let us be
ready for shipping against the time our
Lord's wind and tide call for us.

THERE ARE INFINITE PLIES[14] IN HIS
love that the saints will never win to unfold.

14 layers, folds in cloth

WHEN I LOOK OVER BEYOND THE line and beyond death, to the laughing side of the world, I triumph, and ride upon the high places of Jacob: howbeit, otherways I am a faint, deadhearted, cowardly man, oft borne down and hungry in waiting for the marriage supper of the Lamb. Nevertheless, I think it the Lord's wise love that feeds us with hunger, and makes us fat with wants and desertion.

IT IS LITTLE UP OR LITTLE DOWN that the Lamb and His followers can get, no law-surety nor truce with crosses;[15] it must be so till we are up in our Father's house.

---

15   "no law-surety nor truce with crosses": a Scots phrase corresponding to the English law phrase "being bound over to keep the peace," that is, to give security that one will not use violence towards another against whom one has a grievance. The meaning is that one cannot expect to be immune or untouched by trials and tribulations.

I URGE UPON YOU ... A NEARER communion with Christ and a growing communion. There are curtains to be drawn by in Christ that we never saw, and new foldings of love in Him. I despair that ever I shall win to the far end of that love, there are so many plies in it; therefore dig deep, and sweat, and labour, and take pains for Him, and set by so much time in the day for Him as you can: He will be won with labour.

NEITHER NEED WE FEAR CROSSES, or sigh, or be sad for anything that is on this side of heaven, if we have Christ.

O, THAT WE COULD PUT OUR treasure in Christ's hand, and give Him our gold to keep, and our crown.

OUR FAIR MORNING IS AT HAND,
the day-star is near the rising, and we are
not many miles from home; what matters
the ill entertainment in the smoky inns of
this miserable life? We are not to stay here,
and we will be dearly welcome to Him
whom we go to.

BE PATIENT; CHRIST WENT TO
Heaven with many a wrong. His visage and
countenance was all marred more than the
sons of men. You may not be above your
Master; many a black stroke received in-
nocent Jesus, and He received no mends,[16]
but referred them all to the great court-day,
when all things shall be righted.

16 amends, reparation, righting a wrong

OUT OF WHATEVER AIRT[17] THE wind blow, it will blow us on our Lord: no wind can blow our sails overboard, because Christ's skill and the honour of His wisdom are empawned[18] and laid down at the stake[19] for the seapassengers, that He shall put them safe off His hand on the shore, in His Father's known bounds, our native home ground.

IT IS IMPOSSIBLE TO BE SUBMISSIVE and religiously patient, if ye stay your thoughts down among the confused rollings and wheels of second causes, as O, the place! O, the time! O, if this had been, this had not followed! O, the linking of this accident with this time and place! Look up to the master motion and the first wheel.

17   point of compass, direction
18   pledged
19   staked, pledged

GOD HATH MADE MANY FAIR flowers, but the fairest of them all is heaven, and the flower of all flowers is Christ.

WHEN WE SHALL COME HOME and enter to the possession of our Brother's fair kingdom, and when our heads shall find the weight of the eternal crown of glory, and when we shall look back to pains and sufferings; then shall we see life and sorrow to be less than one step or stride from a prison to glory; and that our little inch of timesuffering is not worthy of our first night's welcome home to heaven.

WE SMELL OF THE SMOKE OF THIS lower house of the earth, because our hearts and our thoughts are here. If we could mount up with God, we should smell of heaven and of our country above, and we should look like our country, and like strangers or people not born or brought up hereaway.[20] Our crosses would not bite upon us, if we were heavenly minded.

LAY ALL YOUR LOADS AND YOUR weights by faith upon Christ. Ease yourself, and let Him bear all. He can, He does, He will bear you.

OUR BEST FARE HERE IS HUNGER.

THIS WORLD DESERVETH NOTHING but the outer court of our soul.

I THINK I SEE MORE OF CHRIST than ever I saw; and yet I see but little of what may be seen.

CHRIST'S CROSS IS SUCH A BURDEN as sails are to a ship or wings to a bird.

20   hereabouts, near this place

WHETHER GOD COME TO HIS children with a rod or a crown, if He come Himself with it, it is well. Welcome, welcome Jesus, what way soever Thou come, if we can get a sight of Thee: and sure I am, it is better to be sick, providing Christ come to the bedside and draw the curtains, and say, Courage, I am thy salvation, than to enjoy health being lusty and strong and never to be visited by God.

THERE ARE MANY HEADS LYING in Christ's bosom, but here is room for yours among the rest.

I AM HALF CONTENT TO HAVE boils for my Lord Jesus's plaisters.[21] Sickness hath this advantage, that it draweth our sweet Physician's hand and His holy

21 plasters, dressings for a wound; hence healings

and soft fingers to touch our withered and leper skins: it is a blessed fever that fetcheth Christ to the bedside—I think my Lord's, "How doest thou with it, sick body?" is worth all my pained nights.

IT IS OUR HEAVEN TO LAY MANY weights and burdens upon Christ.

LET HIM FIND MUCH EMPLOYMENT for His calling with you; for He is such a Friend as delighteth to be burdened with suits and employments; and the more ye lay on Him, and the more homely ye be with Him, the more welcome.

OUR LOVE TO HIM SHOULD BEGIN on earth, as it shall be in heaven; for the bride taketh not by a thousand degrees so much delight in her wedding garment as she doth in her bridegroom; so we, in the life to come, howbeit clothed with glory as with a robe, shall not be so much affected with the glory that goeth about us, as with the Bridegroom's joyful face and presence.

I HOPE YE ARE NOT IGNORANT, that if peace was left to you in Christ's testament, so the other half of the testament was a legacy of Christ's sufferings (John 16:33).

HIS WINDS TURN NOT WHEN HE seemeth to change, it is but we who turn our wrong side to Him.

I AM LIKE A LOW MAN LOOKING up to a high mountain, whom weariness and fainting overcometh. I would climb up, but I find that I do not advance in my journey as I would wish: yet I trust He shall take me home against night.

I THINK IT A SWEET THING, THAT Christ saith of my cross, half mine, and that He divideth these sufferings with me and taketh the largest share to Himself; nay, that I, and my whole cross, are wholly Christ's.

LIVE ON CHRIST'S LOVE WHILE YE are here, and all the way.

FAITH IS EXCEEDING CHARITA-ble, and believeth no evil of God.

YOU MUST LEARN TO MAKE EVILS your great good, and to spin out comforts, peace, joy, communion with Christ, out of your troubles, that are Christ's wooers to speak for you to Himself.

CHRIST'S LOVE, UNDER A VAIL,[22] is love; if ye get Christ, howbeit not the sweet and pleasant way you would have Him, it is enough, for the Well-Beloved cometh not our way.

PUT CHRIST'S LOVE TO THE TRIAL and put upon it burdens, and then it will appear love indeed.

YOUR ROCK DOTH NOT EBB AND flow, but your sea.

THE SEA-SICK PASSENGER SHALL come to land; Christ will be the first that will meet you on the shore.

FAITH LIVETH AND SPENDETH upon our Captain's charges, who is able to pay for all.

22 veil

CHRIST IS AS FULL A FEAST, AS YE can have to hunger.

OUR LORD HUNTETH FOR OUR love, more ways than one or two.

CHRIST HATH COME, AND RUN away to heaven with my heart and my love, so that neither heart nor love is mine.

I SEE CHRIST'S LOVE IS SO KING-ly, that it will not abide a marrow:[23] it must have a throne all alone in the soul.

THE CHILD HATH BUT CHANGED a bed in the garden, and is planted up higher, nearer the sun, where he shall thrive better than in this out-field moor-ground.

23   an equal, a partner

GO ON, AND FAINT NOT, SOMETHING of yours is in heaven, beside the flesh of your exalted Saviour, and ye go on after your own.

HE IS NOT LOST TO YOU WHO IS found to Christ. If he hath casten[24] his bloom and flower, the bloom is fallen in heaven in Christ's lap; and as he was lent awhile to time, so is he given now to eternity, which will take yourself; and the difference of your shipping and his to heaven and Christ's shore, the land of life, is only in some few years, which weareth every day shorter, and some short and soon reckoned summers will give you a meeting with him.

I PRAY YOU LEARN TO BE WORTHY of His pains who correcteth; and let Him wring, and be ye washed; for He hath a Father's heart, and a Father's hand, who is

24 cast, shed, dropped

training you up, and making you meet for the high hall.

ONE YEAR'S TIME OF HEAVEN shall swallow up all sorrows, even beyond all comparison.

FALL DOWN AND MAKE A SURRENDER of those that are gone, and these that are yet alive, to Him. And for you, let Him have all; and wait for Himself, for He will come and will not tarry. Live by faith ... He cannot die whose ye are.

I BESEECH YOU IN THE LORD JESUS, to make every day more and more of Christ, and try your growth in the grace of God, and what ground ye win daily on corruption; for travellers are day by day, either advancing farther on, and nearer home, or else they go not right about to compass their journey.

IT WILL NOT FAIL YOU TO GET two portions, and to laugh twice, and to be happy twice, and to have an upper heaven, and an under heaven too; Christ our Lord and His saints were not so, and therefore let go your grip of this life and of the good things of it. I hope your heaven groweth not hereaway.[25] Learn daily both to possess and miss Christ in His secret Bridegroom smiles; He must go and come, because His infinite wisdom thinketh it best for you. We will be together one day; we shall not need to borrow light from sun, moon, or candle; there shall be no complaints on either side in heaven; there shall be none there but He and we, the Bridegroom and

25 hereabouts, near this place

the bride; devils, temptations, trials, desertions, losses, sad hearts, pain, and death, shall all be put out of play, and the devil must give up his office of tempting. O, blessed is the soul whose hope hath a face looking straight out to that day.

IT IS OUR FOLLY TO DIVIDE OUR narrow and little love. It will not serve two; best then hold it whole and together, and give it to Christ! for then, we get double interest for our love, when we lend it to and lay it out upon Christ; and we are sure besides that the stock cannot perish.

SHE IS NOT SENT AWAY, BUT ONLY sent before, like unto a star, which, going out of your sight, doth not die and vanish, but shineth in another hemisphere: ye see her not yet, she doth shine in another country.

YE ARE NOW YOURSELF ALONE, but ye may have for the seeking, three always in your company, the Father, Son, and Holy Spirit; I trust they are near you.

IF CONTENTMENT WERE HERE, heaven were not heaven.

READ AND SPELL RIGHT, FOR HE knoweth what He doth; He is only lopping and snedding[26] a fruitful tree, that it may be more fruitful.

DO THAT FOR THE LORD WHICH ye will do for time; time will calm your heart at that which God hath done, and let our Lord have it now. What love ye did bear to friends now dead, seeing they stand now in no need of it, let it fall as just legacy to Christ.

26 chopping, pruning, trimming

PUT CHRIST IN HIS OWN ROOM IN your love; it may be He hath either been out of His own place, or in a place of love inferior to His worth.

I WONDER MANY TIMES THAT ever a child of God should have a sad heart, considering what their Lord is preparing for them.

SEND A HEAVY HEART UP TO Christ, it shall be welcome.

I AM PERSUADED, CHRIST IS responsal[27] and lawabiding, to make recompense for anything that is hazarded[28] or given out for Him; losses for Christ are but our goods given out in bank[29] in Christ's hand.

27 responsible, trustworthy, solvent
28 risked
29 lent on trust, literally as a bank loan, as a sum of money to draw upon

I BLESS THE LORD, THAT ALL OUR troubles come through Christ's fingers, and that He casteth sugar among them; and casteth in some ounce weights of heaven and of the spirit of glory in our cup.

TAKE NO HEAVIER LIFT OF YOUR children, than your Lord alloweth; give them room beside your heart, but not in the yolk of your heart, where Christ should be; for then they are your idols, not your bairns. If your Lord take any of them home to His house before the storm come on, take it well, the Owner of the orchard may take down two or three apples off His own trees, before midsummer, and ere they get the harvest sun; and it would not be seemly that His servant, the gardener, should chide Him for it. Let our Lord pluck His own fruit at any season He pleaseth; they are not lost to you, they are laid up so well, as that they are coffered in heaven, where our Lord's best jewels lie.

LET CHRIST HAVE A COMMAND-ing power and a Kingthrone in you.

I FIND HIS SWEET PRESENCE eateth out the bitterness of sorrow and suffering.

TO LIVE ON CHRIST'S LOVE IS A king's life.

IF I COME TO HEAVEN ANY WAY, howbeit like a tired traveler upon my Guide's shoulder, it is good enough for those who have no legs of their own for such a journey. I never thought there had been need of so much wrestling to win to the top of that steep mountain as now I find.

GO UP BEFOREHAND AND SEE your lodging. Look through all your Father's rooms in heaven; in your Father's house are many dwelling-places. Men take a sight of lands ere they buy them. I know Christ hath made the bargain already: but be kind to the house you are going to, and see it often.

ALL THE SAINTS HAVE THEIR own measure of winter before their eternal summer. O! for the long day, and the high sun, and the fair garden, and the King's great city up above these visible heavens! What God layeth on, let us suffer, for some have one cross, some seven, some ten, some half a cross—yet all the saints have whole and full joy, and seven crosses have seven joys.

GLORIFY THE LORD IN YOUR sufferings, and take His banner of love, and spread it over you. Others will follow you, if they see you strong in the Lord; their courage shall take life from your Christian carriage.

THE WEIGHTIEST END OF THE cross of Christ that is laid upon you, lieth upon your strong Saviour.

O, IF I COULD BE MASTER OF THAT house-idol myself, my own, mine, my own will, wit, credit, and ease, how blessed were I! O, but we have need to be redeemed from ourselves rather than from the devil and the world; learn to put out yourselves, and to put in Christ for yourselves.

CHRIST ALL THE SEASONS OF THE
year, is dropping sweetness; if I had vessels I might fill them, but my old riven, hol-
ey, and running-out dish, even when I am
at the well, can bring little away. Nothing
but glory will make tight and fast our leak-
ing and rifty[30] vessels ... How little of the
sea can a child carry in his hand; as little do
I take away of my great sea, my boundless
and running-over Christ Jesus.

SURE I AM HE IS THE FAR BEST
half of heaven; yea He is all heaven, and
more than all heaven.

YE MAY YOURSELF EBB AND FLOW,
rise and fall, wax and wane; but your Lord
is this day as He was yesterday; and it is
your comfort that your salvation is not

30 splitting, unsound

rolled upon wheels of your own making, neither have ye to do with a Christ of your own shaping.

PUT YOUR HAND TO THE PEN, and let the cross of your Lord Jesus have your submissive and resolute Amen.

THE FLOODS MAY SWELL AND ROAR, but our ark shall swim above the waters; it cannot sink, because a Saviour is in it.

LET NOT SALVATION BE YOUR by-work,[31] or your holiday's task only, or a work by the way: for men think, that this may be done in three days' space on a feather-bed, when death and they are fallen in hands together, and that with a word or two they shall make their soul matters

31 spare time

right. Alas, this is to sit loose and unsure in the matters of our salvation.

HOW SOON WILL SOME FEW YEARS pass away, and then when the day is ended, and this life's lease expired, what have men of the world's glory, but dreams and thoughts? O happy soul for evermore, who can rightly compare this life with that long-lasting life to come, and can balance the weighty glory of the one with the light golden vanity of the other.

LAY NO MORE ON THE CREATURES than they are able to carry. Lay your soul and your weights upon God; make Him your only, only best Beloved—your errand in this life is to make sure an eternity of glory to your soul, and to match your soul with Christ; your love, if it were more than all

the love of angels in one, is Christ's due . . .
I know not what ye have if ye want Christ.

IT IS NOT OUR PART TO MAKE A
treasure here: anything under the cover-
ing of heaven we can build upon, is but
ill ground and a sandy foundation: every
good thing, except God, wanteth a bottom,
and cannot stand its alone: how then can it
bear the weight of us?

I WOULD WISH EACH CROSS WERE
looked in the face seven times, and were
read over and over again. It is the messenger of the Lord and speaks something.

TRY WHAT IS THE TASTE OF THE
Lord's cup and drink with God's blessing,
that ye may grow thereby. I trust in God,
whatever other speech it utter to your soul,

this is one word in it, "Behold, blessed is the man whom God correcteth." And that it saith to you, ye are from home while here, ye are not of this world, as your Redeemer Christ was not of this world. There is something keeping for you which is worth the having. All that is here is condemned to die—to pass away like a snowball before a summer sun; and since death took first possession of something of yours, it hath been and daily is creeping nearer and nearer to yourself, howbeit with no noise of feet. Your Husbandman and Lord hath lopped off some branches already, the tree itself is to be transplanted to the high garden. All these crosses are to make you white and ripe for the Lord's harvest hook.

WHAT IS HIS PURPOSE HEREIN, HE knoweth best who hath taken your soul in

tutoring. Your faith may be boldly charita-
ble of Christ, that however matters go, the
worst shall be a tired traveller, and a joyful
and sweet welcome home: the back of your
winter night is broken. Look to the East—
the day sky is breaking; think not that
Christ loseth time or lingereth unsuitably.

IF CHRIST JESUS BE THE PERIOD,
the end and lodging-home, at the end of
your journey, there is no fear, ye go to a
friend . . . . Ye may look death in the face
with joy.

O   WRETCHED   IDOL,   MYSELF!
when shall I see thee wholly decourted,[32]
and Christ wholly put in thy room? O, if
Christ, Christ, had the full place and room
of myself, that all my aims, purposes,

32 excluded from court

thoughts, and desires, would coast and land upon Christ, and not upon myself! And yet, howbeit we cannot attain to this denial of me and mine that we can say I am not myself, myself is not myself, mine own is no longer my own; yet our aiming at this in all we do shall be accepted; for, alas, I think I shall die but minting[33] and aiming to be a Christian.

I AM SURE THE SAINTS AT THEIR best are but strangers to the weight and worth of the incomparable sweetness of Christ. He is so new, so fresh in excellency, every day of new, to these that search more and more in Him, as if Heaven could furnish as many new Christs (if I may speak

---

33 trying to attain perfection; literally making a coin which will be rejected and returned to the melting pot if imperfect.

so) as there are days betwixt Him and us,
and yet He is one and the same.

O, WE LOVE AN UNKNOWN LOVER
when we love Christ.

I THOUGHT IT HAD BEEN AN EASY
thing to be a Christian, and that to seek
God had been at the next door, but oh, the
windings, the turnings, the ups and the
downs that He hath led me through! and I
see yet much way to the ford.

O, WHAT NEED HAVE I TO HAVE THE
ashes blown away from my dying-out fire!
I may be a book-man, and be an idiot and
stark fool in Christ's way; learning will not
beguile Christ: the Bible beguiled the Phar-
isees, and so may I be misted.[34] Therefore,

34 lost in mist, obscured—therefore, led away or
mistaken

as night-watchers hold one another waking by speaking to one another, so have we need to hold one another on foot.

BE NOT AFRAID FOR LITTLE GRACE. Christ soweth His living seed, and He will not lose His seed; if He have the guiding of my stock and state[35] it shall not miscarry. Our spilt works, losses, deadness, coldness, wretchedness, are the ground which the good Husbandman laboureth.

I HAVE HEARD A RUMOUR OF THE prelate's purpose to banish me, but let it come if God so will; the other side of the sea is my Father's ground as well as this side.

LOOK UP TO HIM AND LOVE HIM! O, love and live. Our pride must have winter weather to rot it.

35 possessions and estate

HE HATH MADE ALL HIS PROMIS-
es good to me and hath filled up all the
blanks with His own hand.

I DARE NOT SAY BUT MY LORD JE-
sus hath fully recompensed my sadness with
His joys, my losses with His own presence.
I find it a sweet and rich thing to exchange
my sorrows with Christ's joys, my afflictions
with that sweet peace I have with Him.

PROVIDENCE HATH A THOUSAND
keys to open a thousand sundry doors for
the deliverance of His own, when it is even
come to a *conclamatum est*.[36] Let us be faith-
ful and care for our own part, which is to
do and suffer for Him, and lay Christ's part
on Himself, and leave it there; duties are
ours, events are the Lord's.

---

36   *conclamatum est*—"It is all over" (Latin).

TEMPTATIONS WILL COME, BUT IF
they be not made welcome by you, ye have
the best of it; be jealous over yourself, and
your own heart, and keep touches with
God; let Him not have a faint and feeble
soldier of you; fear not to back Christ, for
He will conquer and over more; let no man
scar at Christ, for I have no quarrels at
His cross. He and His cross are two good
guests, and worth the lodging. Men would
fain have Christ good cheap, but the mer-
cat[37] will not come down. Acquaint yourself with prayer, make Christ your Captain
and your Armour; make conscience of sin-
ning when no eye seeth you.

HE CUTTETH OFF YOUR LOVE TO
the creature, that ye might learn that God
only is the right owner of your love, sorrow,

37 Market price

loss, sadness, death or the worst things
that are, except sin: but Christ knoweth
well what to make of them, and can put
His own in the crosses common, that we
shall be obliged to affliction, and thank
God, who learned us to make our acquaintance with such a rough companion, who
can hale[38] us to Christ.

IT IS EASY TO GET GOOD WORDS
and a comfortable message from our Lord,
even from such rough sergeants as diverse
temptations.

LET US BE GLAD AND REJOICE IN
the salvation of our Lord, for faith had
never yet cause to have wet cheeks and
hanging-down brows, or to droop or die;
what can ail faith, seeing Christ suffereth

38 haul

Himself (with reverence to Him be it spo-
ken) to be commanded by it; and Christ
commandeth all things. Faith may dance
because Christ sings; and we may come in
the quire[39] and lift our hoarse and rough
voices, and chirp, and sing, and shout for
joy with our Lord Jesus.

NONE HAVE RIGHT TO JOY BUT
we, for joy is sown for us, and an ill summer or harvest will not spill[40] the crop.

CHRIST AND HIS CROSS TOGETH-
er are sweet company, and a blessed cou-
ple. My prison is my palace, my losses are
rich losses, my pain easy pain, my heavy
days are holy and happy days. I may tell a
new tale of Christ to my friends.

39 choir
40 spoil

I KNOW MY LORD IS NO NIGGARD:[41]
He can, and it becometh Him well, to give
more than my narrow soul can receive.

IF THERE WERE TEN THOUSAND,
thousand millions of worlds, and as many
heavens full of men and angels, Christ
would not be pinched to supply all our
wants, and to fill us all.

CHRIST IS A WELL OF LIFE, BUT
who knoweth how deep it is to the bottom?

THIS SOUL OF OURS HATH LOVE,
and cannot but love some fair one; and O,
what a fair One, what an only One, what
an excellent, lovely, ravishing One is Jesus.

O, COME ALL AND DRINK AT THIS
living well; come, drink, and live for

41 mean, ungenerous person

evermore; come, drink, and welcome; welcome, saith our fairest Bridegroom: no man getteth Christ with ill will: no man cometh and is not welcome, no man cometh and rueth his voyage: all men speak well of Christ, who have been at Him; men and angels who know Him will say more than I now do, and think more of Him than they can say.

IT SHOULD BE ENOUGH TO ME, IF I were wise, that Christ will have joy and sorrow halfers[42] of the life of the saints, and that each of them should have a share of our days, as the night and the day are kindly partners and halfers of time and take it up betwixt them. But if sorrow be the greediest halfer of our days here, I know joy's day shall dawn, and do more than recompense all our sad hours.

42 sharers of equal parts

I AM IN THIS HOUSE OF MY PIL-
grimage every way in good case; Christ is
most kind and loving to my soul: it pleaseth Him to feast with his unseen consola-
tions a stranger, and an exiled prisoner:
and I would not exchange my Lord Jesus,
with all the comfort out of heaven; His
yoke is easy, and His burden light. This
is His truth I now suffer for; for He hath
sealed it with His blessed presence.

HAPPY ARE THEY WHO ARE FOUND
watching. Our sandglass is not so long as
we need to weary: time will eat away and
root out our woes and sorrow: our heaven
is in the bud, and growing up to an harvest;
why then should we not follow on, seeing
our span-length of time will come to an
inch? Therefore I commend Christ to you as
the Staff of your old age: let Him have now

the rest of your days; and think not much of
a storm upon the ship that Christ saileth in;
there shall no passenger fall overboard; but
the crazed[43] ship and the sea-sick passenger
shall come to land safe.

I AM IN AS SWEET COMMUNION
with Christ as a poor sinner can be; and am
only pained that He hath much beauty and
fairness, and I little love; He great power
and mercy, and I little faith; He much light,
and I bleared eyes.

MY COUNSEL IS, THAT YE COME
out and leave the multitude, and let Christ
have your company. Let them take clay and
this present world who love it: Christ is a
more worthy and noble portion: blessed
are those who get Him.

43   cracked, flawed; in a ship, having weakened timbers

MY DEAR BROTHER, LET GOD
make of you what He will, He will end all
with consolation, and shall make glory out
of your sufferings; and would ye wish better work?

THIS WATER WAS IN YOUR WAY TO
heaven, and written in your Lord's book;
ye behoved to cross it: and therefore kiss
His wise and unerring providence. Let not
the censures of men, who see but the out-
side of things (and scarce well that), abate
your courage and rejoicing in the Lord;
howbeit, your faith seeth but the black side
of providence, yet it hath a better side, and
God shall let you see it.

LEARN TO BELIEVE CHRIST BET-
ter than His strokes; Himself and His
promises better than His glooms .... "For

we know that all things work together for good to them that love God," *ergo*, shipwreck, losses, disappointments, ill tongues, loss of friends, houses or country, are God's workmen, set on work, to work out good to you, out of everything that befalleth you.

LET NOT THE LORD'S DEALINGS seem harsh, rough or unfatherly, because it is unpleasant. When the Lord's blessed will bloweth cross your desires, it is best in humility to strike sail to Him and to be willing to be laid any way our Lord pleaseth: it is a point of denial of yourself, to be as if ye had not a will but had made a free disposition of it to God, and had sold it over to Him; and to make use of His will for your own is both true holiness, and your ease and peace. Ye know

not what the Lord is working out of this,
but ye shall know it hereafter.

VENTURE THROUGH THE THICK OF
all things after Christ, and lose not your Master, Christ, in the throng of this great market.

LET CHRIST KNOW HOW HEAVY,
and how many a stone weight you, and
your cares, burdens, crosses, and sins are;
let Him bear all: make the heritage sure to
yourself: get charters and writs passed and
through,[44] and put on arms for the battle,
and keep you fast by Christ, and then let

---

44   get charters and writs passed and through—a legal
phrase following on the previous clause, "make the
heritage sure to yourself." Heritage is landed property,
houses, etc., which normally descend to the heir-in-
law, who must establish his title to them by producing
the necessary charters and writs (documents), and
getting them approved and "passed and through." So
the meaning is, "Make sure that you will receive the
inheritance of Christ."

the wind blow out of what airt it will, your soul will not blow in the sea.

I FIND CHRIST THE MOST STEAD-able[45] friend and companion in the world to me now: the need and usefulness of Christ is seen best in trials. O, if He be not well worthy of His room! Lodge Him in house and heart.

THERE IS REQUIRED PATIENCE ON our part till the summer fruit in heaven be ripe for us: it is in the bud, but there be many things to do before our harvest come. And we take ill with it, and can hardly endure to set our paper face to one of Christ's storms, and to go to heaven with wet feet, and pain, and sorrow.

45 helpful, available

WE LOVE TO CARRY HEAVEN TO heaven with us, and would have two summers in one year, and no less than two heavens; but this will not be for us: one, and such an one, may suffice us well enough.

THE MAN CHRIST GOT BUT ONE only, and shall we have two?

BE HUMBLED, WALK SOFTLY; down with your topsail. Stoop, stoop! it is a low entry to go in at heaven's gates.

HOWEVER MATTERS GO, IT IS OUR happiness to win new ground daily in Christ's love, and to purchase a new piece of it daily, and to add conquest to conquest, till our Lord Jesus and we be so near each other, that Satan shall not draw a straw or a thread betwixt us.

I DARE AVOUCH[46] TO ALL THAT
know God, that the saints know not the
length and largeness of the sweet earnest,[47]
and of the sweet green sheaves before the
harvest, that might be had on this side of
the water, if we should take more pains:
and that we all go to heaven with less earnest and lighter purses of the hoped for
sum than otherwise we might do, if we
took more pains to win further in upon
Christ in this pilgrimage of our absence
from Him.

I EXHORT YOU IN THE LORD TO
go on in your journey to heaven, and to be
content of such fare by the way as Christ
and His followers have had before you; for
they had always the wind on their faces,

46   vouch for, affirm
47   pledge

and our Lord hath not changed the way to us, for our ease, but will have us following our sweet guide.

O, THAT OUR SOULS WOULD FALL so at odds with the love of this world as to think of it as a traveller doeth of a drink of water, which is not any part of his treasure, but goeth away with the using: for ten miles' journey maketh that drink to him as nothing! O, that we had as soon done with this world, and could as quickly despatch the love of it.

IT COST CHRIST AND ALL HIS followers sharp showers and hot sweats ere they won to the top of the mountain. But still our soft nature would have heaven coming to our bedside when we are sleeping, and lying down with us, that we might go to heaven in warm clothes; but all that came there found wet feet by the way, and sharp storms that did take the hide off their face, and found tos and fros, and ups and downs, and many enemies by the way.

I REJOICE THAT HE IS COME AND hath chosen you in the furnace; it was even there where ye and He set tryst; that is an old gate[48] of Christ's. He keepeth the good old fashion with you, that was in Hosea's days. "Therefore, behold I will allure her, and bring her to the wilderness and speak to her heart" (Hosea 2:14). There was no talking to her heart while He and she were in the fair and flourishing city and at ease; but out in the cold, hungry, waste wilderness, He allureth her, He whispered in news into her ear there, and said, "Thou art mine."

48 habit

WHEN HE WAS IN THE GRAVE, HE came out and brought the keys with Him: He is Lord-jailor: nay, what say I? He is Captain of the castle, and He hath the keys of death and hell: and what are our troubles but little deaths? and He, who commandeth the great castle, commandeth the little also.

THERE BE MANY CHRISTIANS, most like unto young sailors, who think the shore and the whole land doth move, when the ship and they themselves are moved; just so, not a few do imagine that God moveth, and saileth, and changeth places, because their giddy Souls are under sail, and subject to alteration, to ebbing and flowing; but the foundation of the Lord abideth sure.

GOD KNOWETH THAT YE ARE HIS own. Wrestle, fight, go forward, watch, fear, believe, pray; and then ye have all the infallible symptoms of one of the elect of Christ within you.

ACQUAINT YOURSELF WITH Christ's love, and ye shall not miss to find new goldmines and treasures in Christ.

I AM JUST LIKE A MAN WHO HATH nothing to pay his thousands of debt; all that can be gotten of him, is to seize upon his person. Except Christ would seize upon myself, and make the readiest payment that can be of my heart and love to Himself, I have no other thing to give Him.

EVERY MAN THINKETH HE IS RICH enough in grace till he take out his purse and tell his money, and then he findeth his pack but poor and light in the day of a heavy trial. I found I had not to bear my expenses, and should have fainted if want and penury had not chased me to the storehouse of all.

ALAS, THAT WE SHOULD LOVE BY measure and weight, and not rather have floods and feasts of Christ's love! O, that Christ would break down the old narrow vessels of these narrow and ebb souls, and make fair, deep, wide, and broad souls, to hold a sea and a full tide, flowing over all its banks of Christ's love.

YE MUST TAKE A HOUSE BESIDE THE Physician: it shall be a miracle if ye must be the first sick man He put away uncured, and worse than He found you. "Him that

cometh to Me, I will in no wise cast out."
Take ye that; it cannot be presumption to
take that as your own, when ye find your
wounds stound[49] you . . . . Faith hath sense
of sickness, and looketh like a friend to the
promise; and looking to Christ therein, is
glad to see a known face.

IT MAKETH NOT MUCH WHAT WAY
we go to heaven; the happy home is all,
where the roughness of the way shall be for-
gotten. He is gone home to a friend's house,
and made welcome, and the race is ended.

LOOK FOR CROSSES, AND WHILE
it is fair weather mend the sails of the ship.

LET CHRIST'S LOVE BEAR MOST
court in your soul, and that court will bear
down the love of other things.

49 pain

CHRIST CHARGETH ME TO BELIEVE His daylight at midnight.

A HEART OF IRON AND IRON DOORS will not hold Christ out. I give Him leave to break iron locks and come in, and that is all.

I HAVE MANY A GRIEVED HEART daily in my calling. I would be undone, if I had not access to the King's chamber of presence, to show Him all the business.

IT WERE A WELL-SPENT JOURNEY, to creep hands and feet, through seven deaths and seven hells, to enjoy Him up at the well-head. Only let us not weary: the miles to that land are fewer and shorter than when we first believed; strangers are not wise to quarrel with their host, and complain of their lodging; it is a foul way, but a fair home.

DEAR BROTHER, WEARY NOT OF
my sweet Master's chains; we are so much
the sibber[50] to Christ that we suffer. Lodge
not a hard thought of my royal King. Rejoice in His cross. Your deliverance sleep-
eth not. He that will come is not slack of
His promise. Wait on for God's timeous[51]
salvation, ask not when or how long. I hope
He shall lose nothing of you in the furnace,
but dross.

I RATHER WISH HIM MY HEART
than give Him it; except He take it and put
Himself in possession of it (for I hope He
hath a market-right to me, since He hath
ransomed me), I see not how Christ can
have me. O, that He would be pleased to be
more homely with my soul's love, and to
come in to my soul and take His own.

50 more akin, in closer relationship
51 timely

HIS WELL DONE IS WORTH A shipful of good-days and earthly honours.

NOT ONE OUNCE, NOT ONE GRAIN-weight more is laid on me than He hath enabled me to bear ... Faith hath cause to take courage from our very afflictions; the devil is but a whetstone to sharpen the faith and patience of the saints. I know He but heweth and polisheth stones for the new Jerusalem.

HIS CROSS IS THE SWEETEST BUR-den that ever I bare: it is such a burden as wings are to a bird, or sails to a ship, to carry me forward to my harbour.

YE HAVE GOD'S PROMISE, THAT ye shall have His presence in fire, water, and in seven tribulations.

COME IN, COME IN TO CHRIST, AND see what ye want, and find it in Him. He is the short cut (as we use to say) and the nearest way to an outgate[52] of all your burdens. I dare avouch, ye shall be dearly welcome to Him; my soul would be glad to take part of the joy ye should have in Him.

I DARE SAY, ANGELS' PENS, ANgels' tongues; nay, as many worlds of angels as there are drops of water in all the seas, and fountains, and rivers of the earth, cannot paint Him out of you.

BE CONTENT TO WADE THROUGH the waters betwixt you and glory with Him, holding His hand fast; for He knoweth all the fords. Howbeit ye may be ducked, yet ye cannot drown, being in His company. Be

52 outlet

not afraid, therefore, when ye come even to the black and swelling river of death to put in your foot and wade after Him; the current, how strongsoever, cannot carry you down; the Son of God, His death and resurrection, are stepping stones and a stay to you; set down your feet by faith upon these stones and go through as on dry land; if ye knew what He is preparing for you, ye would be too glad.

I DARE NOT THANK MYSELF, BUT I dare thank God's depth of wise providence, that I have an errand in me, while I live, for Christ to come and visit me, and bring with Him His drugs and His balm.

I BUT MAR HIS PRAISES; NAY, I know no comparison of what Christ is, and what His worth is: all the angels, and all the glorified, praise Him not so much as in halves: who can advance Him or utter all His praises?

I KNOW NO SWEETER WAY TO heaven, than through free grace and hard trials together, and one of these cannot well want another.

CHRIST SHOULD BE OUR NIGHT song and our morning song.

BLESSED BE MY RICH LORD JESUS, who sendeth not away beggars from His house with a toom dish. He filleth the vessels of such as will come and seek. We might beg ourselves rich (if we were wise), if we could but hold out our withered hands to Christ, and learn to suit and seek, ask and knock.

I AM EVERY WAY IN GOOD CASE, both in soul and body; all honour and glory be to my Lord. I want nothing but a further revelation of the beauty of the unknown Son of God.

I BESEECH YOU IN THE LORD JESUS, beware, beware of unsound work, in the matter of your salvation: ye may not, ye cannot, ye do not want Christ. Then after this day convene all your lovers before your soul; and give them their leave, and strike hands with Christ, that thereafter there may be no happiness to you but Christ; no hunting for anything but Christ; no bed at night (when death cometh) but Christ: Christ, Christ, who but Christ? I know this much of Christ, He is not ill to be found, not lordly of His love; woe had been my part of it for evermore, if Christ

had made a dainty of Himself to me; but
God be thanked, I gave nothing for Christ;
and now I protest, before men and angels,
Christ cannot be exchanged; Christ cannot
be sold, Christ cannot be weighed.

BECAUSE I AM HIS OWN (GOD BE
thanked) He may use me as He pleaseth.

"IN ALL THEIR AFFLICTIONS HE
was afflicted." Then Christ bore the first
stroke of this cross: it rebounded off Him
upon you, and ye got it at the second hand,
and He and ye are halvers in it. And I shall
believe for my part, He mindeth to distil
heaven out of this loss, and all others the
like; for wisdom devised it, and love laid it
on, and Christ owneth it as His own, and
putteth your shoulder only beneath a piece
of it.

AMONG MANY MARKS[53] THAT WE
are on the journey, and under sail towards
heaven, this is one, when the love of God
so filleth our hearts that we forget to love
and care too much for the having or want-
ing of other things; as one extreme heat
burneth out another.

FOR THIS CAUSE GOD'S BAIRNS
"take well with spoiling of their goods,"
"knowing in themselves, that they have
in heaven a better and an enduring sub-
stance." What better and wiser course can
ye take than to think that your one foot is
here and your other foot in the life to come,
and to leave off loving, desiring, or griev-
ing for the wants that shall be made up
when your Lord and ye shall meet.

53 signs

LET OUR LORD'S SWEET HAND square us and hammer us, and strike off the knots of pride, self-love and world-worship, and infidelity, that He may make us stones and pillars in His Father's house (Rev. 3:12). Think ye much to follow the Heir of the crown, who had experience of sorrows and was acquainted with grief (Isa. 53:3).

WE SEE GOD'S DECREES WHEN they bring forth their fruits, all actions, good and ill, sweet and sour, in their time; but we see not presently the after birth of God's decree, to wit, His blessed end, and the good that He bringeth out of His holy and spotless counsel. We see His working, and we sorrow; the end of His counsel and working lieth hidden and underneath the ground, and therefore we cannot believe.

EVEN AMONGST MEN, WE SEE hewn stones, timber, and a hundred scattered parcels and pieces of a house, all under tools, hammers, and axes, and saws; yet the house, the beauty and ease of so many lodgings and easerooms, we neither see nor understand for the present; these are but in the mind and head of the builder as yet. We see red earth, unbroken clods, furrows, and stones; but we see not summer lilies, roses, and the beauty of a garden.

GIVE HIM LEAVE TO TAKE HIS own way of dispensation with you; and though it be rough, forgive Him; He defieth you to have as much patience to Him, as He hath borne to you ... When His people cannot have a providence of silk and roses, they must be content with such an one as He carveth out for them.

YE WOULD NOT GO TO HEAVEN but with company, and ye may perceive that the way of those who went before you was through blood, suffering, and many afflictions; nay, Christ, the Captain, went in over the door-threshold of paradise, bleeding to death ... Christ hath borne the whole complete cross, and his saints bear but bits and chips; as the apostle saith, "the remnants of leavings of the cross."

I FIND CHRIST TO BE CHRIST, AND that He is far, far, even infinite heaven's height above man. And that is all our happiness. Sinners can do nothing but make wounds that Christ may heal them; and make debts, that He may pay them; and make falls, that He may raise them; and make deaths, that He may quicken them; and spin out and dig hells to themselves, that He may ransom them.

NOW I WILL BLESS THE LORD that ever there was such a thing as the free grace of God, and a free ransom given for sold souls; only, alas! guiltiness maketh me ashamed to apply to Christ, and to think it pride in me to put out my unclean and withered hand to such a Saviour!

BUT IT IS NEITHER SHAME NOR pride for a drowning man to swim to a rock, nor for a ship-broken soul to run himself ashore upon Christ.

WE TAKE IN GOOD PART THAT pride, that beggars beg from the richer. And who is so poor as we? And who is so rich as He who selleth fine gold (Rev. 3:18)?

BE CONTENT, YE ARE HIS WHEAT growing in our Lord's field. And if wheat,

ye must go under our Lord's threshing in-
strument, in His barn-floor, and through
His sieve, and through His mill to be
bruised, as the Prince of your salvation, Jesus, was (Isa. 53:10), that ye may be found
good bread in your Lord's house.

A KING FROM HEAVEN HATH SENT
for you; by faith He showeth you the new
Jerusalem, and taketh you alongst in the
Spirit through all the ease-rooms and
dwelling-houses in heaven, and saith, "All
these are thine, this palace is for thee and
Christ"; and if ye only had been the chosen
of God, Christ would have built that one
house for you and Himself. Now it is for
you and many also.

HE BREAKETH NOT A BRUISED
reed, nor quencheth the smoking flax: but

if the wind blow, He holdeth His hands about it till it rise to a flame.

I AM MOST GLADLY CONTENT that Christ breaketh all my idols in pieces: it hath put a new edge upon my blunted love to Christ. I see He is jealous of my love, and will have all to Himself.

THEY ARE BLESSED WHO SUFFER and sin not, for suffering is the badge that Christ hath put upon His followers: take what way we can to heaven, the way is edged up with crosses . . . . One thing by experience my Lord hath taught me, that the waters betwixt this and heaven may all be ridden, if we be well horsed, I mean, if we be in Christ, and not one shall drown by the way.

NOW WOULD TO GOD, ALL COLD-
blooded,[54] fainthearted soldiers of Christ
would look again to Jesus and to His love;
and when they look, I would have them to
look again and again, and fill themselves
with beholding of Christ's beauty; and I
dare say then, that Christ should come in
great court and request with many.

LIGHTEN YOUR HEART BY LAYING
your all upon Him . . . . Frame yourself for
Christ, and gloom not upon His cross.

I HAVE A LOVER, CHRIST, AND
yet I want love for Him. I have a lovely
and desirable Lord, who is love-worthy,
and who beggeth my love and heart, and
I have nothing to give Him. Dear brother,
come further in on Christ, and see a new

54 having cold feet, cowardly

treasure in Him: come in, and look down, and see angel's wonder, and heaven and earth's wonder of love, sweetness, majesty, and excellency in Him.

DRY WELLS SEND US TO THE fountain.

CHRIST HATH SO HANDSOMELY fitted for my shoulders this rough tree of the cross, as that it hurteth me no ways. My treasure is up in Christ's coffers; my comforts are greater than ye can believe; my pen shall lie for penury of words to write of them.

NO PEN, NO WORDS, NO IMAGE can express to you the loveliness of my only, only Lord Jesus.

TO MISTRESS TAYLOR

Mistress,

Grace, mercy, and peace be to you. Though I have no relation worldly, or acquaintance with you, yet (upon the testimony and importunity of your elder son now at London, where I am, but chiefly because I esteem Jesus Christ in you to be in place of all relations) I make bold in Christ to speak my poor thoughts to you concerning your son lately fallen asleep in the Lord (who was sometime under the ministry of the worthy servant of Christ, my fellow-labourer, Mr. Blair, and by whose ministry I hope he reaped no small advantage).

I know grace rooteth not out the affections of a mother, but putteth them on His wheel who maketh all things new, that they may be refined; therefore sorrow for a dead child is allowed to you, though by measure and ounce-weights; the redeemed of the Lord have not a dominion or lordship over their sorrow and other affections, to lavish out Christ's goods at their pleasure. "For ye are not your own, but bought with a price"; and your sorrow is not your own, nor hath He redeemed you by halves; and therefore ye are not to make Christ's cross no cross.

He commandeth you to weep; and that princely One, who took up to heaven with Him a man's heart to be a compassionate High Priest, became your fellow and companion on earth, by weeping for the dead (John 11:35). And therefore ye are to love that cross, because it was once on Christ's shoulders before you; so that by His own practice He hath overgilded and covered your cross with the Mediator's lustre. The cup ye drink was at the lip of sweet Jesus, and He drank of it; and so it hath a smell of His breath. And I conceive ye love it not the worse that it is thus sugared; therefore drink, and believe the resurrection of your son's body ....

I was not a witness to his death, being called out of the kingdom; but ye shall credit those whom I do credit, he died comfortably. It is true, he died before he did so much service to Christ on earth, as I hope and heartily desire your son Mr. Hugh (very dear to me in Christ) shall do. But that were a matter of sorrow, if this were not to counterbalance it, that he hath changed service-houses,[55] but hath not changed services or Master (Rev. 22:3). What he could have done in this lower house, he is now upon that same service in the higher house; and it is all one, it is the same service, and the same Master, only there is a change of conditions.

55   has changed places of employment

And ye are not to think it a bad bargain for your beloved son, where he hath gold for copper and brass, eternity for time.

I believe Christ hath taught you (for I give credit to such a witness of you as your son Mr. Hugh) not to sorrow because he died. All the knot[56] must be, he died too soon, he died too young, he died in the morning of his life, this is all; but sovereignty must silence your thoughts.

I was in your condition; I had but two children, and both are dead since I came hither. The supreme and absolute Former of all things giveth not an account of any of His matters.

The good husbandman may pluck His roses and gather in His lilies at midsummer, and, for ought I dare say, in the beginning of the first summer month; and He

56 difficulty

may transplant young trees out of the lower ground to the higher, where they have more of the sun, and a more free air, at any season of the year.

What is that to you or me? the goods are His own. The Creator of time and winds did a merciful injury (if I dare borrow the word) to nature in landing the passenger so early.

They love the sea too well who complain of a fair wind and a desirable tide, and a speedy coming ashore, especially a coming ashore in that land where all the inhabitants have everlasting joy upon their heads. He cannot be too early in heaven; his twelve hours were not short hours.

And withal, if ye consider this, had ye been at his bed-side, and should have seen Christ coming to him, ye would not, ye could not, have adjourned Christ's free love, who would want him no longer.

And dying in another land, where his mother could not close his eyes, is not much. Who closed Moses' eyes? and who put on his winding sheet? For ought I know, neither father, nor mother, nor friend, but God only. And there is as expedite, fair, and easy a way betwixt Scotland and heaven, as if he had died in the very bed he was born in. The whole earth is his Father's; any corner of his Father's house is good enough to die in.

It may be, the living child (I speak not of Mr. Hugh) is more grief to you than the dead. Ye are to wait on, if at any time God shall give him repentance; Christ waited as long possibly on you and me, certainly longer on me ....

It seemeth that Christ will have this world your step-dame; I love not your condition the worse; it may be a proof that ye are not a child of this lower house, but a

stranger. Christ seeth it not good only, but
your only good, to be led thus to heaven;
and think this a favour, that He hath be-
stowed upon you free, free grace, that is
mercy without hire, ye paid nothing for it.
And who can put a price upon anything of
royal and princely Jesus Christ? And that
God hath given to you to suffer for Him the
spoiling of your goods, esteem it as an act
of free grace also; ye are no loser, having
Himself; and I persuade myself if ye could
prize Christ, nothing could be bitter to you.
Grace, grace be with you.

> Your brother and well-wisher,
> S. R.
> London, 1645

TO THE LADY EARLSTOUN

Mistress,

Grace, mercy, and peace be to you. I long to hear how your soul prospereth. I exhort you to go on in your journey; your day is short, and your afternoon's sun will soon go down; make an end of your accounts with your Lord; for death and judgment are tides that bide no man.

Salvation is supposed to be at the door, and Christianity is thought an easy task, but I find it hard, and the way strait and narrow, were it not but my guide is content to wait on me, and to care for a tired traveller.

Hurt not your conscience with any known sin; let your children be as so many flowers borrowed from God; if the flowers die or wither, thank God for a summer's loan of them, and keep good neighbourhood to

borrow and lend with Him. Set your heart
upon heaven, and trouble not your spirit
with this clay idol of the world, which is
but vanity, and hath but the lustre of the
rainbow in the air, which cometh and goeth
with a flying March shower . . . .

My Lord hath made me well content of
a borrowed fireside, and a borrowed bed. I
am feasted with the joys of the Holy Ghost,
and my royal King beareth my charges
honourably . . . .

The great messenger of the covenant, the
Son of God, establish you on your rock, and
keep you to the day of His coming.

> Yours in his sweet Lord Jesus,
> Samuel Rutherford.
> Aberdeen, March 7, 1637

FOR MARION M'KNAUGHT

Loving and dear Sister,

I fear that you be moved and cast down because of the late wrong that your husband received in your town-council; but I pray you comfort yourself in the Lord, for a just cause bides under the water only as long as wicked men hold their hands above it; their arm will weary, and then the just cause shall swim above, and the light that is sown for the righteous shall spring and grow up.

If ye were not strangers here, the dogs of the world would not bark at you. You shall see all the windings and turnings that are in your way to heaven out of God's word; for He will not lead you to the kingdom at the nearest; but you must go through (2 Cor. 6:8) "honour and dishonour, by evil report

and good report, as deceivers and yet true";
verse 9, "as unknown and yet well-known,
as dying and behold we live, as chastened
and not killed"; verse 10, "as sorrowful and
yet alway rejoicing."

The world is one of the enemies that we
have to fight with, but a vanquished and
overcome enemy, and like a beaten and
forlorn soldier; for our Jesus hath taken the
armour from it: let me then speak to you in
His words. "Be of good courage," saith the
Captain of our salvation, "for I have overcome the world."

You shall neither be free of the scourge of
the tongue, nor of disgraces, even if it were
buffetings and spittings upon the face, as was
our Saviour's case, if you follow Jesus Christ.

I beseech you in the bowels of our Lord
Jesus, keep a good conscience (as I trust
you do); you live not upon men's opinions;

gold may be gold and have the king's stamp upon it, when it is trampled upon by men.

Happy are you if, when the world trampleth upon you in your credit and good name, yet you are the Lord's gold, stamped with the King of heaven's image, and "sealed by His Spirit unto the day of your redemption." Pray for the Spirit of love (1 Cor. 13:7). Love "beareth all things, believeth all things, hopeth all things, endureth all things."

And I pray you that your husband, yea I charge you before God and the Lord Jesus Christ, and the elect angels, pray for these your adversaries: read this to your husband from me; and let both of you "put on, as the elect of God, bowels of mercies."

And, sister, remember how many thousands of talents of sins your Master hath forgiven you: forgive ye, therefore, your fellow-servants one talent; follow God's command in this, "and seek not after your own heart, and after your own eyes" in this matter, as the Spirit speaks (Num. 15:39).

Ask never the counsel of your own heart here; the world will blow up your heart now, and cause it swell, except the grace of God cause it to fall. Jesus, even Jesus, the eternal Wisdom of the Father, give you wisdom; I trust God shall be glorified in you; and a door shall be opened unto you as the Lord's prisoners of hope, as Zechariah speaks.

It is a benefit to you that the wicked are God's fan to purge you; and I hope they shall blow away no corn or spiritual graces, but only your chaff. I pray you, in your pursuit, have so recourse to the law of men that you wander not from the law of God. Be not cast down: if you saw Him, who is standing

on the shore, holding out His arms to welcome you to land, you would not only wade
through a sea of wrongs, but through hell
itself, to be at Him: and I trust in God you
see Him sometimes. The Lord Jesus be with
your spirit, and all yours.

Your brother in the Lord,

S. R.

Anwoth.

YE HAVE ONLY THESE TWO SHALLOW
brooks, sickness and death, to pass through;
and ye have also a promise that Christ
shall do more than meet you, even that He
shall come Himself, and go with you, foot
for foot, yea and bear you in His arms. O
then! for the joy that is set before you, for
the love of the Man (Who is also God over
all, blessed forever) that is upon the shore to
welcome you: run your race with patience.